# SOLAR SYSTEM GUIDEBOOK

Ruth Strother

Silver Dolphin

**Silver Dolphin Books**
An imprint of Printers Row Publishing Group
A Division of Readerlink Distribution Services, LLC
10350 Barnes Canyon Road, Suite 100, San Diego, CA 92121
www.silverdolphinbooks.com

ISBN: 978-1-62686-306-4
Manufactured, printed, and assembled in Shaoguan, China.
First Edition
19 18 17 16 15    1 2 3 4 5

Written by Ruth Strother
Designed by Dynamo, Ltd.
Reviewed by Andrew K. Johnston,
Geographer for the Center for
Earth and Planetary Studies,
National Air and Space Museum,
Smithsonian

For Smithsonian Enterprises:
Chris Liedel, President
Carol LeBlanc, Senior Vice President, Education and Consumer Products
Brigid Ferraro, Vice President, Education and Consumer Products
Ellen Nanney, Licensing Manager
Kealy Gordon, Product Development Manager, Licensing

Photo Credits          Key: c = center, t = top, b=bottom, l = left, r = right
**Book Front Cover:** Shutterstock: 3Dsculptor, Johan Swanepoel, ArchMan, Thinkstock: Photodisc, iStock: Sergey Volkov, m-gucci, Alexey Kuzin **Book Back Cover:** Shutterstock: Johan Swanepoel, dimitris_k, Denis Kuvaev, Thinkstock: Stockbyte: Comstock Images, iStock: surlyaslisaksom, George Toubalis **Tin Interior:** Thinkstock: iStock: leonello, Shutterstock: mozzyb, Tjeffersion, Alhovik, **Tin Exterior:** Shutterstock: 3Dsculptor, Johan Swanepoel, ArchMan, Gl0ck, dimitris_k, Thinkstock: Stocktrek Images, Photodisc, iStock: Sergey Volkov, m-gucci, Alexey Kuzin, forplayday, George Toubalis **Magnets:** Thinkstock: Stocktrek Images, Stockbyte, Purestock, Photodisc: NASA, Hemera: Tyler Olson, iStock: m-gucci, yganko, MarcelC, James Thew, Alexey Kuzin, STILLFX, suriyasilsaksom, Shutterstock: Edwin Verin, Nerthuz, NASA **Clings:** Thinkstock: Purestock, Stocktrek Images, Getty Images: Sergii Tsololo, Stockbyte: Comstock Images, iStock: Sergey Volkov, m-gucci, Nettedotca, valeriopardi, suriyasilsaksom, GEORGE TOUBALIS, Ben-Schonewill Creativemarc, Shutterstock: Edwin Verin **Book Interior:** NASA: 6cr, 18br, 21br, 31l, 33tr, 47, 47c, 48cr, 49cr, 50br, 58br, 61bl / SuperStock, Inc.: 11bl, Heinz-Dieter Falkenstein: age fotostock 53br, Dieter Spannknebel: Exactostock-1491 54cl, NASA: age fotostock 59tr, StockTrek: 60c, Purestock 56c, NASA 49cl, 57cl, Science and Society 48br, 45tl, Ctein 52tr, Exactostock-1527 58bl, Tony Hallas 55bl, DeAgostini 60cr, Everett Collection 44cr, Fine Art Images 44bl, fStop 45bl / Thinkstock: purestock 1br, 8bl, Stockbyte 2br, Comstock Images 64br, Stocktrek Images 7bl, 17tr, 25tr, 25c, 27tl, 27c, 29, 37, 59cl, Hemera: Andrea Danti 5c, 16tc, 24tc, 26tc, 28tc, 30tc, 32tc, 34tc, 36tc, 38tc, 63c, Dmitriy Eremenkov 16br, Adrian Hillman 18cr, Paul Moore 51cl, Monkey Business Images 10bl, Design Pics 23br, 49tl, C 33, Purestock 35, 45tr, Goodshoot 45br, Wetcake Studio 22bl, Zoonar: Zoonar 3br, Photodisc: Digital Vision 53tr, iStock: 22cr, somchaisom 1bc, 5br, egal 4cr, 12c, Sergey Volkov 4bl, 17bl, Yuriy Mazur 6b, GEORGE TOUBALIS 7cl, 15br, David Szabo 7cr, yganko 20cr, Joe Rainbow 23br, 62c, 39, 60cr PapaBear 26cr, Lars Lentz 34cr, m-gucci 40cr, 41, 63tl, Lars Lentz 47b, valeriopardi 53bl, PaulFleet 54cr, Neutronman 55br, suriyasilsaksom 62bl, leonello 64br / Shutterstock: clearviewstock 1b, 2b, 3b, 14b, 15b, G10ck 3tr, 5bc, 62tl, pixelparticle 4b, 5b, 11b, 18b, 19b, 24b, 25b, 38b, 39b, atribut 4, 5, 6tl, 7tl, 8br, 9tr, 11br, 13tr, 14, 15, 17, 18br, 19, 20cl, 21, 22br, 23tl, 24, 25, 26br, 27, 28, 29, 31, 33, 35, 37, 38, 39, 41, 48, 49, 52bl, 53br, 55, 58cl, 60br, 61cl, 44br, 45br, Attitude: 5bl, 9bl, 10br, 15cr, 17cl, 19cr, 21bl, 23tr, 24br, 27bl, 29tr, 30, 33, 35tr, 37bl, 38br, 40br, 41bl, 43tl, 46cr, 47, 49, 50cr, 51tl, 53tl, 54bl, 55br, 57tl, 59, 60c, Kjpargeter 5br, 17br, 18cl, 21tr, 23cl, 30cr, 32br, 49tr, 51tr, 55cl, 56br, 58cr, 61br, 45bl, Bildagentur Zoonar GmbH 6b, 7b, 12b, 13b, Fred Fokkelman 8b, 9b, Iculig 9tl, Champion Studio 9br, Michelangelus 10b, 11tr, donatas1205 10tl, 12t, 16tc, 18, 20tc, 22tc, 24tc, 25tc, 28, 30tc, 32, 34br, 36, 38, 40, 42, 46tc, 48tc, 50, 52tc, 54tc, 56tc, 58tc, 60tc, 44tc, 62tl, 64tl, Johan Swanepoel 13cr, 22b, 23b, 64t, Filipe Frazao 13bl, BlueRingMedia 14c, cherezoff 14bl, Maria Starovoytova 16b, 17b, 26b, 27b, AAR Studio 17br, LingHK 18bl, andrey_l 18br, sciencepics 19tr, Catmando 19b, agsandrew 20b, 21b, 63br, AstroStar 20bl, Vadim Sadovski 21tr, 34b, 35b, jupeart 21bl, 30b, 31b, 36b, 37b, 63tr, R-studio 22tl, 24, 34, 62b, 63b, 64b, jonson 23tl, Juergen Faelchle 23cr, 62br, MarcelClemens 28b, 28bc, 29b, 55c, IM_photo 28b, Webspark 29tr, Elenarts 31tl, 51cr, SergeyDV 31br, tuntekron petrajun 32b, 33b, Tristan3D 33bc, dezignor 35bc, 3drenderings 36br, whitehoune 39tr, Igor Kovalchuk 40b, 41b, 59br, mejnak 42b, 43b, Paul Reeves Photography 43tc, Aaron Rutten 46b, 47b, 49b, Anatoliii Vasilev 48b, Diego Barucco 49cr, Andrea Danti 50b, 51b, Triff 50cl, vector photo video 52b, 53b, 62tr, Muskola Stock Photos 54b, 55b, 2happy 55tc, Paul Fleet 56b, 57b, Stefano Garau 58b, 59b, John A Davis 60b, b, Viktar Malyshchyts 60bl, inigocia 61, HelenField 44b, 45b

# TABLE OF CONTENTS

# WHAT IS THE SOLAR SYSTEM?

One of the first things you notice when you step outside in the morning is the Sun. Is it shining brightly and warming the air? Is it hiding behind clouds? The Sun doesn't just help us decide whether to wear a jacket, it's also at the center of our **solar system**. In fact, the word solar means "of the Sun."

The Sun is made of gas and the same elements found in planets. The planets, dwarf planets, **asteroids, comets,** and **meteoroids** were made from what was left over after the Sun formed.

## THE SUN IS THE STAR

Even though at night we see hundreds of stars decorating our sky, only one star is actually in our solar system. That star is the Sun. The Sun's gravity pulls everything else in the solar system onto a path around it. Planets, dwarf planets, moons, rocky asteroids, icy comets, and meteoroids are some of the celestial bodies trapped by the Sun's gravity.

## THE TERRESTRIAL PLANETS

Mercury, Venus, Earth, and Mars are the four planets closest to the Sun and the smallest planets in our solar system. They are called **terrestrial** planets because their surface is rocky and solid.

## THE GAS GIANTS

Jupiter, Saturn, Uranus, and Neptune are called gas giants, and they are farther from the Sun than the terrestrial planets. Gas giants are made mostly of hydrogen and helium gases with some water and other gases in the mix. **Astronauts** can't land on these planets because their gassy makeup doesn't form a solid surface.

SUN

JUPITER

SATURN

NEPTUNE

EARTH

MARS

URANUS

VENUS

MERCURY

## MOONS

Moons are natural objects that orbit, or circle, planets. Some planets have many moons, and some have none. Earth has one Moon.

## ASTEROIDS, COMETS, AND METEOROIDS

Asteroids are large rocks that **orbit** the Sun. Comets orbit the Sun too, but they are made of dust and rocks trapped in frozen liquid. Think of them as dirty snowballs in space. Meteoroids are space rubble made of rocks and metals like iron and nickel.

Our solar system is about 4.6 billion years old.

# WHERE IN THE WORLD?

The universe holds everything we can see, measure, or touch. It is full of planets, solar systems, and galaxies. Our solar system is just a tiny part of our **galaxy**, which is only a tiny part of the **universe**.

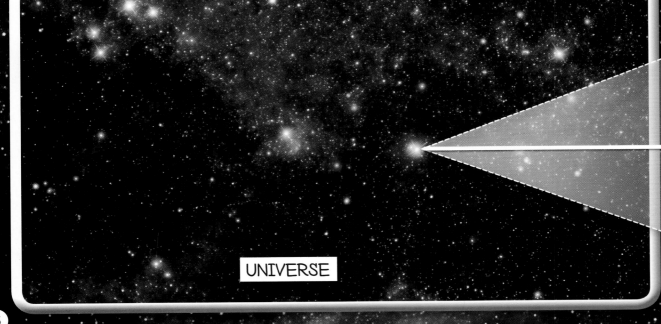

UNIVERSE

Another word for the universe is the cosmos.

SOLAR SYSTEM

EARTH

GALAXY

# HOW THE SOLAR SYSTEM WORKS

Every object in the universe that has **mass** pulls other objects toward it. This force is called **gravity.** Gravity keeps you grounded on Earth so you don't float off into space. It's also what makes apples fall from trees.

Mass is the amount of matter, or stuff, in an object.

## GRAVITATIONAL PULL

The size of the objects and the distance between them determine the strength of the gravitational pull. You have a gravitational force that affects everything and everyone around you. Your force isn't strong, though, because you aren't massive. A really big object such as the Sun or Earth has a very strong gravitational force.

## MICROGRAVITY

The floating feeling you have on a roller coaster when it seems your stomach has been left behind is the same feeling of weightlessness that astronauts feel in outer space. You feel like you're floating because you are falling along with your seat. In orbit, this is called microgravity.

Because of microgravity, people can't cry in space. Astronauts can tear up, but the tears remain on the eye as a ball of liquid.

## WEIGHT AND MASS

Your mass stays the same no matter which planet you're on. But how much you weigh is a combination of your mass and how strong gravity is where you are. So if you weigh 60 pounds on Earth, you would weigh just under 23 pounds on Mars, but you would weigh just over 152 pounds on Jupiter!

# ORBITING THE SUN

The Sun is so huge that its gravitational pull reaches out trillions of miles into space. And that pull makes Earth and other planets orbit the Sun. So how is it that little Earth isn't gobbled up by the giant Sun? While the Sun's gravity is pulling Earth toward it, Earth is traveling fast enough that it can't be pulled into the Sun. Instead, Earth orbits the Sun.

SUN

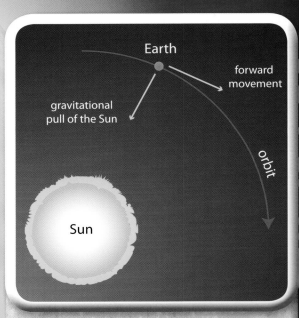

Earth

forward movement

gravitational pull of the Sun

orbit

Sun

Earth has its own force of gravity that pulls us, its **atmosphere**, and everything else on the planet toward its center. When we jump, it's gravity that pulls us back to the ground and keeps us from flying into space.

## IT'S LIKE THIS . . .

Think of a tennis ball on a string. Hold onto the end of the string while spinning in a circle, and the ball will swing out in a circle around you. The string acts like the gravitational pull of the Sun, but the forward movement of the ball keeps it swinging around. This balance of gravity and forward movement keeps the planets in our solar system orbiting around the Sun.

EARTH

PATH OF ORBIT

## BENDING SPACE

Albert Einstein came up with a new way of thinking about space, time, and gravity. He didn't think the Sun's gravity was pulling space objects into orbit. Instead, he thought that objects caused the space around them to curve. The Sun, being big, causes a curve so steep that it forces other objects like planets to follow the curve and go into orbit. Careful observations have since confirmed Einstein's theories.

# REVOLUTION

The amount of time it takes a planet to complete a full circle, or **revolution**, around the Sun is how we define one year. Earth takes 365 days, 6 hours, and 7 seconds to circle the Sun. Earth's revolution, together with its **rotation**, creates the seasons.

The Earth speeds around the Sun at about 67,000 miles per hour!

How many Earth days or years does it take each planet to complete one revolution around the Sun?

**MERCURY:** 88 DAYS      **JUPITER:** 12 YEARS

**VENUS:** 225 DAYS      **SATURN:** 29.5 YEARS

**EARTH:** 1 YEAR      **URANUS:** 84 YEARS

**MARS:** 687 DAYS      **NEPTUNE:** 165 YEARS

An orbit is the path of a planet, moon, comet, or spacecraft around another body, such as a planet, moon, or the Sun. A revolution is the completion of an orbit.

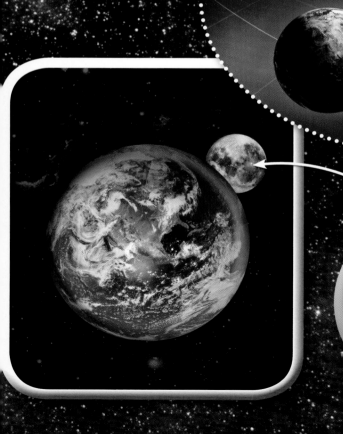

The Moon revolves around Earth. It takes about 27 days for the Moon to complete one revolution.

# AXIS AND ROTATION

## AXIS

Imagine an invisible line running through the center of Earth from North Pole to South Pole. This "line" is called the **axis**. Earth rotates around this axis every day. All planets have an axis.

NIGHT    DAY

## ROTATION

Earth rotates around its axis like a spinning globe. At the same time, it orbits the Sun. As Earth rotates, certain parts of it face the Sun, making it daytime there. The other side of Earth is facing away from the Sun, making it nighttime. All planets spin around their axis, but they do so at varying speeds.

How many Earth days or hours does it take each planet to complete one rotation around its axis?

| | |
|---|---|
| **MERCURY:** 59 EARTH DAYS | **JUPITER:** 10 HOURS |
| **VENUS:** 243 EARTH DAYS | **SATURN:** 10 HOURS |
| **EARTH:** 1 EARTH DAY | **URANUS:** 17 HOURS |
| **MARS:** 1 EARTH DAY | **NEPTUNE:** 16 HOURS |

Mercury has a slow rotational speed, so any given spot on the planet will be in sunlight for about three months, and then in darkness for three months.

## THE SEASONS

Earth's axis is tilted. The tilt causes the North Pole to point toward and away from the Sun at different times of the year. When Earth's northern half leans toward the Sun, it gets more sunlight. The days are longer and warmer. The southern half, then, is leaning away from the Sun, making the days shorter and colder. After six months, Earth leans the other way, and the seasons are reversed.

## CLOCKWISE OR COUNTERCLOCKWISE?

Venus and Uranus are the only planets that rotate in a clockwise direction as seen from above the Sun's north pole. All the other planets rotate in a counterclockwise direction. Scientists think that objects may have collided into Venus and Neptune to change the direction of their rotation.

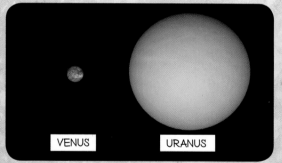

VENUS          URANUS

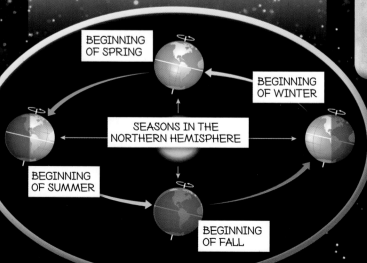

BEGINNING OF SPRING

BEGINNING OF WINTER

SEASONS IN THE NORTHERN HEMISPHERE

BEGINNING OF SUMMER

BEGINNING OF FALL

Every planet in our solar system has a North Pole and a South Pole because every planet rotates on its axis.

# THE SUN

The Sun is a hot star and the only star in our solar system. It holds the solar system together with its gravitational pull. The Sun is about 4.3 billion years old, and it's expected to continue burning for another 5 to 7 billion years.

Another word for Sun is Sol.

It takes 8 minutes for light from the Sun to reach Earth.

The Sun is so huge that one million Earths would fit inside it!

## HOW MUCH MASS?

Mass is the amount of matter or stuff in an object. The larger the mass of an object, the stronger the gravitational pull. The Sun has the most mass in our solar system. Even though there are eight planets, the Sun makes up a whopping 99.86 percent of the solar system's mass.

## GASSY ENERGY

The Sun, like all stars, is made mostly of two gassy elements: helium and hydrogen. The force of gravity squeezes the gases into a hot ball and turns the hydrogen into helium. This makes the Sun give off heat and light.

## SOLAR ERUPTIONS

A solar flare, or solar eruption, is an explosion of energy in the Sun's atmosphere. The most powerful flares can cause spacecraft orbiting the Earth to stop working correctly.

## SUNSPOTS

Sunspots are dark, cool spots on the Sun's surface caused by solar storms. Sunspots are still bright, but they are dimmer than the rest of the Sun. A single sunspot can be many times bigger than Earth, but you need a telescope to see one from Earth.

# STARS

Stars appear to us as tiny pinpricks of light. But if you could travel trillions of miles through space to get a closer look, you would see that they are enormous. Stars are hot, brightly burning balls of gas. They can burn for billions of years.

## GIANT STARS

Giants, supergiants, and hypergiants are the biggest stars. They are millions of miles across, really bright, and cooler than many stars. Giant stars are between ten and a few thousand times brighter than the Sun.

The closest star to Earth is our Sun, of course. The closest star to our Sun is very far away. It takes four years for its light to reach us here on Earth.

## RED GIANTS

Red giants are huge stars, usually 30 times the size of the Sun. Late in their life, red giants shrink into white dwarfs.

A black dwarf is a frozen lump of carbon, which is like coal.

## DWARF STARS

Dwarf stars are smaller stars like our Sun. Red dwarfs are the most common kind of star in our galaxy. They are smaller and cooler than the Sun.

## WHITE DWARFS

White dwarfs are tiny hot stars about the size of Earth. A white dwarf drifts and cools in space for thousands of years. Eventually, it cools completely and becomes a black dwarf drifting through space.

The Earth's Sun is a common, average-sized star called a yellow dwarf. The Sun's yellow color comes from the surface temperature, which is about 9,900 degrees Fahrenheit.

## NEUTRON STARS

Neutron stars are only about the size of a city. A neutron star may be small, but it has a giant mass. A piece of a neutron star the size of one board-game die weighs as much as all the people on Earth put together.

If you dropped a single spoonful of neutron star material over Earth it would fall like a rock and bore a hole through the whole planet—in one side and out the other!

# THE LIFE AND DEATH OF A STAR

Stars are constantly being squeezed by the force of gravity. This makes them release a lot of energy that we see as bright starlight. Usually after billions of years, stars begin to run low on fuel. That's when they grow to be giants or supergiants. After a while, they run out of fuel completely and die.

The brightest stars in our sky seem to form patterns and shapes. If you connect the bright dots with imaginary lines, you can see shapes that look like people and animals. We call these patterns **constellations**.

How a star dies depends on what type of star it is. Most stars become dwarfs. Some huge stars explode as an amazing **supernova**.

Many different kinds of stars dot our sky. They vary in brightness, color, mass, size, and speed of travel through space.

## NEBULAE

Nebulae are clouds of hydrogen gas and dust that are lit by stars. They may be the leftovers of exploded stars. The hot gases can join together to form new stars and even planets.

## AGING STARS

Stars look different from each other depending on their age and temperature. Stars that look red are cooler. They burn fuel slowly so they can last a long time. Stars with a bright blue-white color are hotter. They burn their fuel faster so they might not live as long.

## SUPERNOVAS

A supernova is the explosion of a gigantic star that has grown old and run out of fuel. The explosion is bright and powerful. It hurls a huge amount of star matter into space. A supernova is so bright that it can outshine all of the stars in its galaxy. But it soon fades from sight.

The Cat's Eye Nebula has a striking bull's-eye pattern. Scientists believe that the rings of dust around the Cat's Eye Nebula were created by explosions that were about 1,500 years apart.

# THE SUN AND EARTH

The Sun's light and warmth is what makes life on Earth possible. It provides energy that we can use in many ways. Plants get energy from the Sun. Animals get energy by eating plants or by eating other animals that have eaten plants.

## THE CYCLE OF WATER

The Sun helps water evaporate into the atmosphere, where it forms clouds and then rains back down to Earth. This is an important system called the water cycle.

The Sun's diameter is its width from one side to the other. It's about 100 times bigger than Earth's diameter. You would need to line up 100 Earths to reach across the diameter of the Sun!

## SOLAR ENERGY

We can capture the Sun's energy and turn it into power. We use the power to heat and cool our homes, run our electrical appliances, and even drive our cars.

## SOLAR ECLIPSE

A solar **eclipse** happens when the Moon passes between Earth and the Sun. The Moon blocks the light of the Sun from reaching Earth. All we can see from Earth is light from the Corona, a zone of glowing gases around the Sun.

*Never look directly at a solar eclipse, because it will damage your eyes.*

## ASTRONOMICAL UNIT

The Earth travels on an elliptical, or oval, orbit around the Sun. This makes the distance between Earth and the Sun vary from 91 to 94 million miles. The average distance between the Earth and the Sun is called an Astronomical Unit (AU).

## AURORAS

Earth is surrounded by a magnetic field that protects us from the Sun's rays and wind. Solar eruptions can mix with Earth's magnetic field and create beautiful light shows called **auroras**. In the northern hemisphere, these lights are called aurora borealis. Auroras have been seen on Jupiter, Saturn, and Uranus, planets that also have magnetic fields.

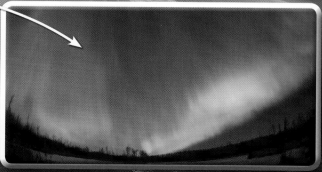

# TERRESTRIAL PLANETS: MERCURY

Mercury is the closest planet to the Sun, but the least explored of the terrestrial planets. It is hard to see from Earth because it is hidden by the Sun's glare. The best time to see Mercury from Earth is right before the Sun rises and again just after it sets.

## MERCURY FACT FILE

**LENGTH OF DAY:** 58 EARTH DAYS, 15 HOURS

**LENGTH OF YEAR:** 88 EARTH DAYS

**AVERAGE DISTANCE FROM THE SUN:** 35,980,000 MILES

**DIAMETER AT EQUATOR:** 3,032 MILES

**NUMBER OF MOONS:** 0

**SURFACE DETAILS:** EXTREMELY THIN ATMOSPHERE, ROCKY TERRAIN WITH RIDGES, CLIFFS, LARGE AREAS THAT ARE HEAVILY CRATERED, AND AREAS THAT ARE ALMOST CRATER-FREE.

**MADE OF:** ROCKS AND A HUGE IRON CORE

**TEMPERATURE:** RANGES FROM -300°F AT NIGHT TO 800°F DURING THE DAY

## LONG DAYS

Mercury rotates very slowly. Any given spot on the planet is in sunlight for about three months, and then in darkness for about three months. But its orbit around the Sun is the smallest of all the planets, which allows Mercury to complete a revolution in only 88 Earth days.

## NO AIR OR ATMOSPHERE

Mercury barely has an atmosphere so the sky is always black. The temperatures swing from being extremely hot during the day to being bitterly cold at night. Although helium, oxygen, and sodium exist on the planet's surface, powerful winds send these gases out to space. So Mercury is pretty much airless.

Mercury has very little atmosphere to protect it, which means that its surface is covered with impact **craters**.

## CRATERS

Mercury looks a lot like our Moon. It is a dry, rocky planet with huge cliffs and craters. The largest of its craters, the Caloris Basin, is about 800 miles across.

Mercury is 70 percent iron, making it the most iron-rich planet in the solar system. Its iron core is about the size of our Moon.

Even though Mercury is the closest planet to the Sun, it's not the hottest—Venus is.

# TERRESTRIAL PLANETS:
# VENUS

Venus is the second planet from the Sun and the closest planet to Earth. It is scorchingly hot, and the air is full of deadly acid. Its sky is yellow and filled with strange clouds and lightning. From Earth, Venus is the brightest-looking planet in the sky.

## VENUS FACT FILE

**LENGTH OF DAY:** 243 EARTH DAYS

**LENGTH OF YEAR:** 225 EARTH DAYS

**AVERAGE DISTANCE FROM THE SUN:** 67,240,000 MILES

**DIAMETER AT EQUATOR:** 7,521 MILES

**NUMBER OF MOONS:** 0

**SURFACE DETAILS:** HOT, DRY ROLLING PLAINS WITH SOME MOUNTAINS AND NO CRATERS

**MADE OF:** A CENTRAL IRON CORE AND A ROCKY MANTLE, SIMILAR TO THE COMPOSITION OF EARTH. ITS ATMOSPHERE IS MADE UP OF 96 PERCENT CARBON DIOXIDE, 3 PERCENT NITROGEN, AND A SMALL AMOUNT OF OTHER GASES.

**AVERAGE TEMPERATURE:** 864°F

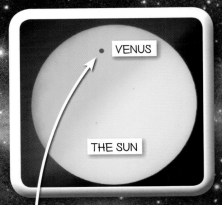

VENUS

THE SUN

## TRANSIT OF VENUS

A transit of Venus is when Venus passes between the Sun and Earth. For a short time Venus becomes visible against the background of the Sun. During a transit, Venus can be seen from Earth as a small black dot moving across the face of the Sun.

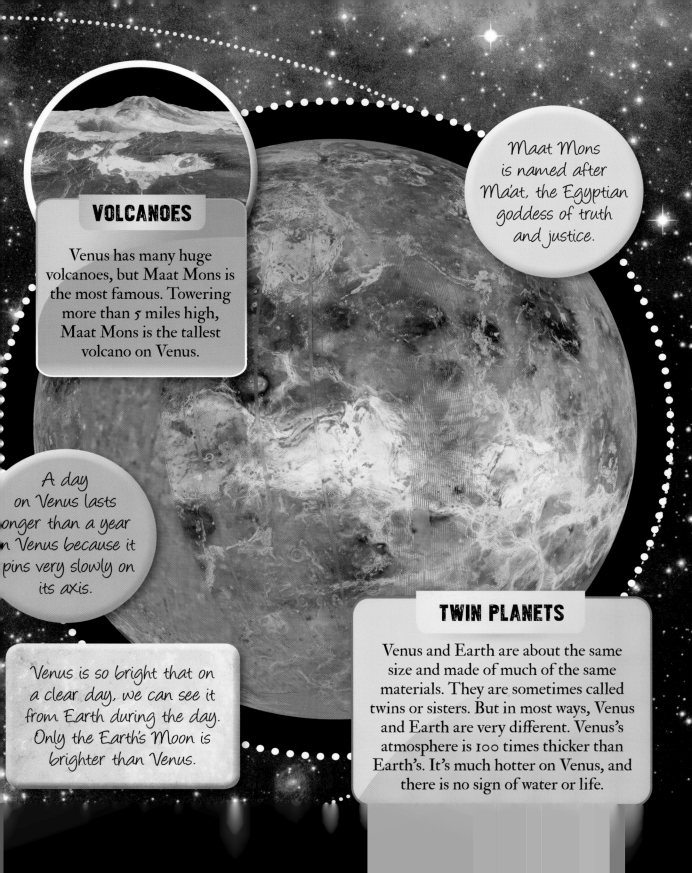

## VOLCANOES

Venus has many huge volcanoes, but Maat Mons is the most famous. Towering more than 5 miles high, Maat Mons is the tallest volcano on Venus.

Maat Mons is named after Ma'at, the Egyptian goddess of truth and justice.

A day on Venus lasts longer than a year on Venus because it spins very slowly on its axis.

Venus is so bright that on a clear day, we can see it from Earth during the day. Only the Earth's Moon is brighter than Venus.

## TWIN PLANETS

Venus and Earth are about the same size and made of much of the same materials. They are sometimes called twins or sisters. But in most ways, Venus and Earth are very different. Venus's atmosphere is 100 times thicker than Earth's. It's much hotter on Venus, and there is no sign of water or life.

# TERRESTRIAL PLANETS: EARTH

Earth is the third planet from the Sun. It is home to more than 30 million different forms of life. Most of Earth's surface is covered with water, so it looks blue when seen from space. Life on Earth is made possible by the right combination of air, water, and warmth from the Sun.

## EARTH FACT FILE

**LENGTH OF DAY:** 23 HOURS, 56 MINUTES, AND 4 SECONDS

**LENGTH OF YEAR:** 365.25 DAYS

**AVERAGE DISTANCE FROM THE SUN:** 92,960,000 MILES

**DIAMETER AT EQUATOR:** 7,926.28 MILES

**NUMBER OF MOONS:** 1

**SURFACE DETAILS:** ABOUT 70 PERCENT IS COVERED WITH WATER, AND 30 PERCENT IS COVERED WITH ROCK, SOIL, AND PLANTS.

**MADE OF:** METALS, MINERALS, AND WATER

**TEMPERATURE:** AVERAGE OF 58.2°F

## THE EARTH'S ATMOSPHERE

Our atmosphere protects Earth from meteorites and blocks out deadly radiation. It gives us the air we breathe. It is mostly made up of nitrogen and oxygen, but it also has some carbon dioxide, water vapor, and other gases.

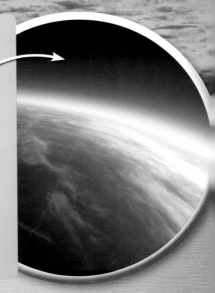

Water is one of the main reasons Earth can support life.

## THE CRUST

The crust is the top layer of the Earth. It's the layer we live on. Even though oceans cover about 70 percent of the surface, Earth is made mostly of granite and basaltic rock.

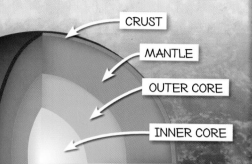

CRUST
MANTLE
OUTER CORE
INNER CORE

## THE MANTLE

Right under the crust is a layer of very hot, dense rock called the mantle. This layer of rock is so hot that it flows like asphalt, a sticky black liquid we use to make roads.

## THE OUTER CORE

Earth's third layer is the outer core made of the metals nickel and iron. The outer core is so hot that these metals have melted into a liquid.

## THE INNER CORE

In Earth's center is the inner core. The temperature in the inner core is thought to be a whopping 9,800°F! It's so hot and the pressure is so high that the liquid metals are squeezed together and forced into a solid form.

The liquid iron in the outer core spins, making Earth a giant magnet. This is where we get the names North Pole and South Pole. It is also why compasses work.

# TERRESTRIAL PLANETS: MARS

Mars is the fourth planet from the Sun. Its soil is filled with iron-rich minerals that rust because of the Martian air. The rust makes the soil look red, which gives Mars its nickname, the Red Planet.

## MARS FACT FILE

**LENGTH OF DAY:** 24 HOURS, 40 MINUTES

**LENGTH OF YEAR:** 687 EARTH DAYS

**AVERAGE DISTANCE FROM THE SUN:** 141,600,000 MILES

**DIAMETER AT EQUATOR:** 4,212 MILES

**NUMBER OF MOONS:** MARS HAS TWO MOONS, NAMED PHOBOS AND DEIMOS.

**SURFACE DETAILS:** A ROCKY SOLID SURFACE THAT HAS BEEN SHAPED BY VOLCANOES, IMPACTS FROM SPACE OBJECTS, AND DUST STORMS.

**MADE OF:** A CORE OF MAINLY IRON AND SULFUR AND A SURFACE OF BASALT AND JUST ENOUGH IRON OXIDE TO GIVE THE PLANET ITS REDDISH HUE

**TEMPERATURE:** HIGH TEMPERATURES OF 70°F AT NOON AT THE EQUATOR IN THE SUMMER, WITH A LOW TEMPERATURE OF ABOUT -225°F AT THE POLES

## DUST STORMS

The dry Martian surface gets churned up by winds, creating massive dust storms that cover the planet and can rage for more than a month.

## WATER ON MARS

Scientists think that billions of years ago, Mars may have been warmer and wetter, more like Earth. But over time, Mars's atmosphere became thinner, and the planet became much colder. The only water left on Mars is frozen at the poles or hidden in deep underground springs.

## VOLCANOES AND MOUNTAINS

Like Earth, Mars has frozen north and south poles. It also has gigantic volcanoes that are no longer active. Mars's Olympus Mons is about 15 miles high, making it the tallest volcano and mountain in the solar system.

Mars's Olympus Mons is three times taller than Earth's Mount Everest!

## VALLEYS AND CANYONS

Mars has deserts with canyons and the longest and deepest valley in the solar system. Valles Marineris is 6 miles deep in parts and stretches for 2,500 miles.

Scientists want to explore Mars because it may have once been more like Earth. Evidence of past life may be waiting to be found.

Valles Marineris was named after the Mariner 9 space probe, which discovered it in 1971. A space probe collects information to send back to Earth.

# GAS GIANTS: JUPITER

## JUPITER FACT FILE

**LENGTH OF DAY:** 10 HOURS

**LENGTH OF YEAR:** 12 EARTH YEARS

**AVERAGE DISTANCE FROM THE SUN:** 483,800,000 MILES

**DIAMETER AT EQUATOR:** 86,881 MILES

**NUMBER OF MOONS:** AT LEAST 67 (4 LARGE MOONS, AT LEAST 63 OTHERS)

**SURFACE DETAILS:** ITS ATMOSPHERE IS MADE UP OF MOSTLY HYDROGEN GAS AND HELIUM GAS, AND THE SURFACE IS COVERED IN THICK RED, BROWN, YELLOW, AND WHITE CLOUDS.

**MADE OF:** MOSTLY HYDROGEN AND HELIUM, WITH A POSSIBLE MOLTEN CORE

**TEMPERATURE:** IN THE CLOUDS OF JUPITER THE AVERAGE TEMPERATURE IS -234°F, BUT AT THE PLANET'S CORE IT IS AS HOT AS 43,000°F, WHICH IS HOTTER THAN THE SURFACE OF THE SUN!

Jupiter is the fifth planet from the Sun. It is one of the gas giants and is the largest and most massive planet in the solar system. It is also the fastest-spinning planet in the solar system.

## THE GREAT RED SPOT

Jupiter is famous for a huge storm that has been raging on its surface for over 500 years. Called the Great Red Spot, this storm is showing signs of weakening. It once measured 25,000 miles in diameter. Now it's only a bit bigger than Earth at just under 10,000 miles in diameter.

## VACUUM CLEANER OF THE SOLAR SYSTEM

People call Jupiter the solar system's vacuum cleaner because it pulls in comets and **meteors**. Scientists believe that if it weren't for Jupiter, about 10,000 times more space objects would be slamming into Earth.

## 67 MOONS AND COUNTING

Jupiter holds the record for the planet with the most moons in our solar system, with at least 67 moons. The moon Io has more than 150 volcanoes. Europa has an icy surface that may cover a saltwater ocean. Ganymede is the largest moon in our solar system.

## JUPITER'S RING

In 1979 a faint ring around Jupiter was discovered. Scientists saw three parts to the ring: one main part made up mostly of dust, a faint inner part known as a halo, and an even fainter sheer ring that lies beyond the main ring.

A day on Jupiter is only about 10 hours long.

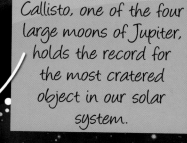

Callisto, one of the four large moons of Jupiter, holds the record for the most cratered object in our solar system.

# GAS GIANTS:
# SATURN

Saturn is the sixth planet from the Sun, and it is the most distant planet that we can see with the naked eye from Earth. Saturn has the most spectacular ring system of any planet in our solar system.

## SATURN FACT FILE

**LENGTH OF DAY:** 10 HOURS, 32 MINUTES

**LENGTH OF YEAR:** 29.5 EARTH YEARS

**AVERAGE DISTANCE FROM THE SUN:** 890,700,000 MILES

**DIAMETER AT EQUATOR:** 74,732 MILES

**NUMBER OF MOONS:** AT LEAST 62 (1 LARGE AND 6 MEDIUM-SIZED MOONS, AT LEAST 55 OTHERS)

**SURFACE DETAILS:** GAS

**MADE OF:** HYDROGEN WITH LESSER AMOUNTS OF HELIUM. IT MOST LIKELY HAS A THICK ATMOSPHERE AND A SMALL, ROCKY CORE SURROUNDED BY A LIQUID.

**TEMPERATURE:** -285°F

## STUNNING RINGS

Saturn's ring system is made up of seven individual rings. They are named A through G in the order they were discovered. The brilliant icy rings are made of dust and billions of rock pieces. They range from tiny, dust-sized icy grains to a few that are as large as mountains.

## A HUGE BALL OF GAS

Saturn is a humongous ball of gas, mostly hydrogen and helium. Like Jupiter, Saturn doesn't have a surface you can walk on. That's why it's called a gas giant.

Jupiter, Uranus, and Neptune have rings, but they aren't as big and bright as Saturn's.

Saturn's density is so low that if you could drop it into water, it would float!

## AN ORBIT OF RINGS

Saturn's rings may have formed by pieces of comets, asteroids, or shattered moons that broke up before they reached the planet. Instead of hitting the planet, they were caught up in Saturn's orbit.

The winds on Saturn can reach 1,118 miles per hour. Compare that to Earth, where the strongest winds may reach 250 miles per hour.

# GAS GIANTS: URANUS

Uranus is the seventh planet from the Sun. It looks like a green pea when you look at it through a small telescope. Through a more powerful telescope, the planet looks like a glowing blue-green orb. The color comes from the methane gas in its atmosphere.

## URANUS FACT FILE

**LENGTH OF DAY:** 17.9 HOURS

**LENGTH OF YEAR:** 84.3 EARTH YEARS

**AVERAGE DISTANCE FROM THE SUN:** 1,787,000,000 MILES

**DIAMETER AT EQUATOR:** 31,800 MILES

**NUMBER OF MOONS:** AT LEAST 27 (5 LARGE MOONS, AT LEAST 22 OTHERS)

**SURFACE DETAILS:** LARGE, ROCKY CORE WITH A SURFACE OF GASES AND ICE MADE OF METHANE, HYDROGEN, AND HELIUM

**MADE OF:** FROZEN GASES AND A MOLTEN CORE. ITS ATMOSPHERE IS MADE OF 83 PERCENT HYDROGEN, 15 PERCENT HELIUM, AND 2 PERCENT METHANE

**AVERAGE TEMPERATURE:** -357°F NEAR THE CLOUD TOPS

### RINGS AROUND THE PLANET

In 1997, scientists first spotted a band of rings around Uranus. Today, 15 faint rings have been discovered. The inner rings are narrow and dark; the outer rings are brightly colored.

Uranus is eight times larger than Earth.

## ICE GIANT

Uranus cannot support life as we know it. The planet is a gas giant and does not have a solid surface. Most of Uranus is made up of hot, dense fluid topped by ammonia and methane ices. That's why it's called the ice giant.

The closest we've come to Uranus was in 1986 when the spacecraft Voyager 2 flew 50,600 miles from it.

## SIDEWAYS PLANET

Unlike any other planet in our solar system, Uranus has a 98-degree tilt to its axis. It rotates on its side! Scientists think that a huge space object may have crashed into Uranus, throwing it onto its side. The planet's north pole now faces the Sun, while its south pole points out into space. That means the north pole gets 42 years of sunlight followed by 42 years of darkness.

# GAS GIANTS: NEPTUNE

Neptune is the eighth planet from the Sun, and the farthest planet ever reached by spacecraft. It is a deep-blue giant with huge, violent storms and unbelievably high winds and cold temperatures.

## NEPTUNE FACT FILE

**LENGTH OF DAY:** 16 HOURS, 6 MINUTES

**LENGTH OF YEAR:** 164.79 EARTH YEARS

**AVERAGE DISTANCE FROM THE SUN:**
2.8 BILLION MILES

**DIAMETER AT EQUATOR:** 30,599 MILES

**NUMBER OF MOONS:** AT LEAST 14
(1 LARGE MOON, AT LEAST 13 OTHERS)

**SURFACE DETAILS:** GASES

**MADE OF:** VERY COLD HYDROGEN, HELIUM, AND METHANE GASES AND ICE WITH A ROCKY CORE

**TEMPERATURE:** -353°F

## WILD WEATHER

Like Uranus, Neptune is an ice giant. Besides its freezing temperatures, its wild weather includes the strongest winds of any planet in the solar system. Neptune's winds can reach the supersonic speed of 1,300 miles per hour!

## HOT ICE

Beneath its clouds, Neptune has a slushy surface of hot ice. That's right, hot ice! Neptune's heavy atmosphere presses down on the inside of the planet, making the pressure deep inside incredibly high. This high pressure stops ice from melting. The ice can be slushy, and it can actually be hot.

When Voyager 2 passed by Neptune, it was able to confirm that the planet has a faint ring system around it.

## DIAMONDS IN SPACE

Some scientists think that the high pressure on Neptune could be strong enough to squeeze the carbon on the planet into diamonds. If this is true, there could be tiny diamonds falling into the center of the planet!

Since it was discovered in 1846, Neptune has completed only one orbit.

The force of gravity on Neptune is similar to Earth's gravitational force.

# EARTH'S MOON

Astronomers think that a very long time ago, Earth smashed into an object the size of Mars. The collision broke off huge chunks of Earth that were flung into space. Over time the Earth chunks joined and made our Moon.

## LUNAR FACT FILE

**LENGTH OF DAY:** 29.5 EARTH DAYS

**LENGTH OF YEAR:** 27 EARTH DAYS

**AVERAGE DISTANCE FROM THE SUN:** 238,900 MILES

**DIAMETER AT EQUATOR:** 2,159 MILES

**SURFACE DETAILS:** ROCKY, WITH HILLS, MOUNTAINS, AND CRATERS

**MADE OF:** THE CRUST IS MADE MOSTLY OF VOLCANIC MATERIAL. THE SMALL CORE MAY BE METALLIC IRON, SULFUR, AND NICKEL.

**TEMPERATURE:** -243°F TO 253°F

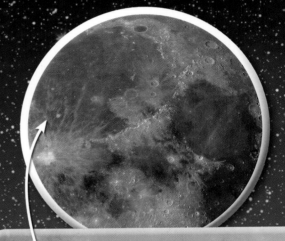

### THE MAN IN THE MOON

When you look at the Moon, you might be able to see what looks like a man's face smiling at you. This image is formed by flat plains called maria. Lava from the eruptions of ancient volcanoes caused the maria, which look like dark blotches. These blotches form the features of a person's face.

Scientists have found indications of frozen water buried in the surface at the Moon's poles. The water may have come from icy comets that crashed into the Moon.

## EVERLASTING FOOTPRINTS

The Moon's surface is covered with dry, sandy dust called regolith. There is no weathering from wind or rain, so the Moon's craters have lasted for billions of years. The footprints left by astronaut Neil Armstrong, the first man to walk on the Moon, will still be there millions of years from now.

## THE FAR SIDE OF THE MOON

The Moon rotates while it orbits, so one side is always facing Earth. That means we see the same side of the Moon all the time. We call it the near side. The far side of the Moon used to be called the dark side of the Moon, not because it is actually dark, but because it was a mystery.

Unlike Earth, the Moon doesn't have an atmosphere to protect it, so meteors and asteroids crash into the Moon, leaving huge craters.

# THE MOON'S CHANGING SHAPE

The Moon's phase describes how much of the Moon we see lit up by the Sun. The Moon is waxing as it moves from new Moon to full Moon, and it's waning as it moves from full Moon to new Moon.

The Moon doesn't shine the way the Sun does. Its light is actually a reflection of light from the Sun. When the Moon's orbit puts it between Earth and the Sun, we don't see much of the Moon at all. This is the new Moon phase. As it moves along in its orbit, more of the Moon becomes visible to us. We see a full Moon when it is on the other side of Earth.

WAXING GIBBOUS

FIRST QUARTER

WAXING CRESCENT

NEW MOON

## LUNAR ECLIPSE

An eclipse happens when a planet, moon, star, or other celestial body passes into the shadow of another celestial body. A lunar eclipse, or an eclipse of the Moon, can happen only when the Moon is full and passing through Earth's shadow. It can last for an hour and a half, and the Moon may look red!

It's not safe to look at a solar eclipse, but you can look at a lunar eclipse without being harmed because the Moon doesn't make its own light.

During a partial lunar eclipse, only part of the Moon passes through Earth's shadow. The whole Moon passes through Earth's shadow during a total lunar eclipse.

FULL MOON

WANING GIBBOUS

LAST QUARTER

WANING CRESCENT

NEW MOON

When two full Moons appear in the same calendar month, the second one is called a blue Moon—but it isn't really blue.

# A RACE TO THE MOON

People have been fascinated with space since the first time someone looked at the night sky. But it wasn't until 1957 that we were actually able to go up there and take a look around. That's when the Soviet Union rocketed Sputnik 1 into Earth's orbit. That same year, the Soviets launched the first Earthling into orbit. She was a dog named Laika.

SPUTNIK 1

Sputnik 1, a beach ball-sized satellite, orbited the planet for only 92 days, but it was a major milestone in space exploration.

Cosmonaut is the Russian word for an astronaut.

## FIRST HUMANS IN SPACE

In 1961, Soviet cosmonaut Yuri Gagarin became the first person to orbit the Earth. Less than a month later, American Alan Shepard made the first pilot-controlled space flight. Then President John F. Kennedy boldly announced that the United States would land a man on the Moon by the end of the decade.

## APOLLO 11

The race to land the first humans on the Moon led to Apollo 11, a spacecraft that carried three astronauts who were soon to make history. On July 20, 1969, two of those astronauts, Neil Armstrong and Buzz Aldrin, became the first humans to set foot on the Moon.

The most famous objects left on the Moon are the astronauts' footprints. Because the Moon has no atmosphere, wind, or water to erase them, these footprints will be around for a very long time.

## WHAT WE LEFT ON THE MOON

The astronauts planted an American flag in the ground to show that people had been on the Moon. They left some other things on the Moon. The most useful item was a 2-foot-wide panel of 100 mirrors pointing toward Earth. Those mirrors are still being used today to learn about the Moon's orbit.

## SPACE EXPLORATION

Many countries are now exploring space. But so far no human has set foot on any other planet or moon in outer space besides our Moon. Better technology and a better understanding of space are allowing us to explore farther out into space than ever before.

# THE MOONS OF MARS

Mars has two moons, Phobos and Deimos. They are two of the smallest moons in our solar system. They're not round like Earth's Moon, but lumpy and uneven. Like Earth's Moon, they have a lot of craters, and one side of both Martian moons always faces the planet.

Phobos orbits Mars three times a day, and Diemos orbits Mars once every 30 hours.

While Phobos is moving closer to Mars, Deimos is moving farther away. Someday it may move so far away from Mars that Deimos will leave Mars's orbit.

Phobos's gravitational pull is so weak that a 150-pound person would weigh a mere 2 ounces!

# THE MOONS OF JUPITER

Jupiter's moon Ganymede is the largest moon in our solar system. If Ganymede orbited the Sun instead of Jupiter, it would be considered a planet!

**Jupiter has the most moons in our solar system with at least 67 known moons.**

**Jupiter has four large moons called the Galilean moons, named after Galileo Galilei, who is credited with discovering the moons in 1610.**

ome of Jupiter's large moons may have oceans under their crusts that could possibly sustain life.

Io is the closest large moon to Jupiter, and it has more than 150 volcanoes.

# THE MOONS OF SATURN, URANUS, AND NEPTUNE

Only 53 of Saturn's moons have been named.

## SATURN'S UNIQUE MOONS

Saturn has at least 62 moons, many with unique characteristics:

- Some of Saturn's moons move in different directions in their orbits.

- Two of Saturn's moons orbit in gaps within its main rings.

- Some small moons actually share one orbit.

- Two of Saturn's moons, Janus and Epimetheus, occasionally pass close to one another and switch orbits periodically.

- One of Saturn's moons has an odd flat shape and rotates chaotically, probably due to a recent collision.

## SATURN'S BIGGEST MOON

Saturn's largest moon is Titan. It was also the first of Saturn's moons to be discovered. It's covered in a thick haze that only certain cameras and telescopes can pierce. When scientists could see through the haze, they were surprised to see liquids on its surface.

TITAN

## THE MOONS OF URANUS

While most moons in our solar system have names from Greek mythology, Uranus's moons are named after characters from the works of William Shakespeare and Alexander Pope.

Uranus has 5 large moons and more than 20 tiny moons, made mostly of ice and rock.

## THE STRANGEST MOON OF URANUS

The closest large moon to Uranus is Miranda. Its canyons are so deep that they make Earth's Grand Canyon look shallow. In fact, Miranda's surface is stranger and more varied than that of any other celestial body.

ARIEL

MIRANDA

## NEPTUNE'S MOONS

Neptune has at least 14 moons. The largest, Triton, is one of the few moons in our solar system that has an atmosphere. It's a thin atmosphere made mostly of methane and nitrogen gases.

Triton is the only large moon to orbit its planet in the opposite direction of its rotation. This is called a retrograde orbit.

TRITON

## THE COLDEST MOON OF NEPTUNE

Triton is Neptune's largest moon. It is one of the coldest places in our solar system, with a temperature of −400°F. It has volcanoes that spew out a mix of methane, liquid nitrogen, and dust that freezes into a snowy flurry as it drops to the moon's surface.

# ASTEROIDS, COMETS, METEOROIDS, AND THE KUIPER BELT

People sometimes confuse asteroids with comets. Comets are made of ice and rock and have tails when they approach the Sun.

Asteroids can be as small as a city block or as big as 400 miles across. They're made of iron and rock much like the terrestrial planets. And they orbit the Sun like planets do. They are so much like planets that the bigger asteroids are sometimes called planetoids or minor planets.

## THE ASTEROID BELT

Our solar system is home to millions of asteroids. Most of them orbit the Sun in a swath between Mars and Jupiter called the asteroid belt.

At least 150 asteroids have a moon, and some even have two moons!

## CERES

The biggest asteroid was also the first asteroid to be discovered. Ceres is about 600 miles across. It's so large that many classify it as a dwarf planet. Ceres is unusual because it's round like a sphere. Most asteroids are irregularly shaped and look more like potatoes.

## CRATERS

When an asteroid crashes into a planet, it creates an impact crater. Many planets and moons, including Earth's Moon, are pockmarked with craters. Only a few craters can be found on Earth because most impacting bodies burn up in the atmosphere.

## OUT OF ORBIT

A planet's gravitational force can pull an asteroid out of orbit. When that happens, the asteroid might become a moon of that planet. Scientists think that Phobos and Deimos were asteroids that were pulled into Mars's orbit. They are now considered to be two of the moons of Mars.

Jupiter's gravitational pull protects Earth, as well as Mercury, Venus, and Mars, from repeated asteroid attacks. When a piece of an asteroid does happen to crash into Earth, it's called a meteorite.

# COMETS

Comets are celestial objects that orbit the Sun. All comets circle the Sun in an elliptical (oval) orbit. They can spend hundreds and thousands of years way out in the farthest reaches of the solar system before their orbit brings them close to the Sun. Like all orbiting objects, the closer they are to the Sun, the faster they move.

## A DIRTY SNOWBALL IN SPACE

The center, or nucleus, of a comet can be up to 10 miles wide. It is made of dust and rocks trapped in frozen liquid. Comets are like dirty snowballs in space! The Sun melts some of the ice, releasing gases and dust particles. The dust and gases reflect the Sun's light, which allows us to see the comet.

We usually don't see a comet until it gets closer to the Sun than Jupiter's orbit.

When a comet is close to the Sun, it gets a fuzzy outline around its head called a coma. That's because ice in the comet's nucleus changes to gas and forms an atmosphere around the comet.

## WHY DO COMETS HAVE TAILS?

The tail of a comet can trail for millions of miles into space. It is a mix of dust and ice. Comets can have two tails: a bluish gas tail and a yellowish dust tail. Solar winds always push the tail away from the Sun, no matter which direction the comet is moving.

Some comet tails stretch as long as the distance between Earth and the Sun!

## HALLEY'S COMET

Halley's Comet was discovered by Isaac Newton and Edmund Halley in 1680. Halley thought that the same comet had been appearing about every 76 years. He predicted that it would return in 1758. He was right. It was named Halley's Comet in his honor. Halley's Comet last passed by Earth in 1986. We will see it again in 2062.

EDMUND HALLEY

# METEOROIDS

Is it a meteoroid? Is it a meteor? Is it a meteorite? No, it's a **shooting star!** Wait. What exactly is the difference? A meteoroid is small space rubble. When a meteoroid enters the Earth's atmosphere, it heats up and glows, becoming a meteor. If the meteor doesn't burn out before hitting Earth, it's a meteorite.

## METEOR

A meteor is rock and debris that has broken off a meteoroid and entered Earth's atmosphere. As it enters Earth's atmosphere, a meteor may streak across the night sky leaving a trail of light in its wake. A falling meteor can be breathtaking to watch.

## METEOR SHOWER

Every so often, Earth's orbit passes through a trail of material left over from a comet. This creates a meteor shower. Meteor showers can be seen in the night sky on almost the same date every year. The most exciting ones happen around January 3, August 12, and December 14.

A meteoroid can travel through space at 26 miles per second!

## METEOROID

A meteoroid orbits the Sun. It is made up of rocks and metals like iron and nickel.

## FIREBALL

A really bright meteor is really a large meteoroid (a few feet in diameter) entering Earth's atmosphere. They're called fireballs. Some fireballs make noise; some shed smaller meteors; some produce sonic booms, which are extremely loud noises; and some leave a trail that can be seen for several minutes.

Large fireball meteoroids are more likely than the smaller ones to survive their fall through the atmosphere and strike Earth's surface.

## METEORITE

Once in a while, a large meteor does not completely burn up in Earth's atmosphere. Instead, the leftover bits smash into Earth. These leftovers are called meteorites. Small meteorites look like dark-colored Earth rocks.

When you wish upon a falling star, you're really wishing upon a meteor!

## CRATERS

Large meteorites have made craters in Earth's surface. The Barringer Crater in northern Arizona was made when a meteorite over 100 feet in diameter smashed into Earth. Many other craters are much larger, but they have eroded.

# THE KUIPER BELT

Just beyond Neptune's orbit is the Kuiper Belt. Scientists think that this area may be home to hundreds of thousands of small ice-covered worlds. These celestial bodies have formed a belt that surrounds and orbits the Sun.

## PLUTO

The most famous object in the Kuiper Belt is Pluto, which was discovered in 1930. Pluto, its moon Charon, and some other very tiny moons orbit the Sun. But they are so far away from the Sun that their surfaces are always cold and dark.

Beyond the Kuiper Belt are even more distant areas of tiny icy bodies called the Scattered Disk and the Oort Cloud.

## THE NINTH PLANET

Until 2006, Pluto was considered to be the ninth planet in our solar system. But scientists discovered many other icy worlds around the same size as Pluto in the Kuiper Belt. Was Pluto really a planet? Nobody had defined what makes a *planet*.

## WHAT IS A PLANET?

Astronomers came up with a definition of a planet. They decided that three conditions are needed for a space object to be called a planet.

1. It must orbit the Sun.
2. It has to be big enough so its gravity forces it into a round shape.
3. It has to be big enough to clear a path for its orbit.

Pluto doesn't meet the third condition.

Today, Pluto is often called a "dwarf planet". Some other dwarf planets are Eris, Makemake, and Haumea.

## KUIPER BELT OBJECTS FACT FILE

**NAME:** PLUTO
**LOCATION:** KUIPER BELT
**FAR-OUT FACT:** PLUTO WAS ONCE CLASSIFIED AS A PLANET.

**NAME:** ERIS
**LOCATION:** KUIPER BELT / SCATTERED DISK
**FAR-OUT FACT:** ERIS HAS A THIN ATMOSPHERE THAT COLLAPSES AND FREEZES AS IT ORBITS FARTHER FROM THE SUN.

**NAME:** MAKEMAKE (MAH-KAY-MAH-KAY)
**LOCATION:** KUIPER BELT
**FAR-OUT FACT:** THE DISCOVERY OF MAKEMAKE AND ERIS LED TO THE NEW CLASSIFICATION OF PLANETS AND DWARF PLANETS.

**NAME:** HAUMEA
**LOCATION:** KUIPER BELT
**FAR-OUT FACT:** HAUMEA ROTATES SO FAST THAT ITS SPIN CAUSED IT TO STRETCH INTO THE SHAPE OF AN OVAL.

# GALAXIES

A galaxy is a collection of stars, gas, dust, and planets all bound together by gravity. Not all galaxies look alike. They are classified into three types based on their shape. Galaxies can be spiral, elliptical, or irregular.

## SPIRAL GALAXY

Galaxies form as a spiral disk. Many maintain a spiral shape as they get older. These spiral galaxies are either ordinary or barred. A barred spiral galaxy has a bar across its center that gives it two major arms.

## PARTS OF A SPIRAL GALAXY

Spiral galaxies have three parts—the bulge, the disk, and the halo. The bulge is round, in the center of the galaxy, and made mostly of old stars. The disk can form arms. It is made of young stars, gas, and dust. The halo is a loose group of old stars around the bulge.

This galaxy, called NGC 1300, is a barred spiral like our home Milky Way galaxy.

SPIRAL GALAXY M81

## ELLIPTICAL GALAXY

Elliptical galaxies are older than spiral galaxies. Some elliptical galaxies are created when nearby galaxies collide and get squished into an oval-shaped disk.

Elliptical is another way to say oval.

## IRREGULAR GALAXY

Irregular galaxies have no spiral or elliptical structure. They do have a lot of dust that hides their stars from us. Irregular galaxies are probably shaped by how their gravity interacts with other galaxies. It basically messes up their nice clean spiral shape.

## SMALLEST AND BIGGEST

The smallest galaxies known are called dwarf galaxies. These galaxies may contain as few as 10 million stars. The largest known galaxy is Andromeda, which contains about 1,000 billion stars.

ANDROMEDA

## GALAXY CLUSTER

Galaxies cluster into huge groupings much like stars gather into galaxies. Within a galaxy cluster, each galaxy orbits the cluster's center of mass the way planets orbit their sun.

There can be billions of stars in one galaxy and there may be hundreds of billions of galaxies in the universe.

# THE MILKY WAY

The Milky Way is where we live but it is just one among billions of spiral-shaped galaxies in the universe. The Milky Way galaxy spans about 100,000 light-years across, and it is about 10,000 light-years thick.

MILKY WAY

A **light-year** isn't a unit of time; it's a measure of distance. A light-year is the distance that light travels in one year, which is about 5.88 trillion miles.

## OUR SOLAR SYSTEM IN THE MILKY WAY

The Milky Way has two major arms and two minor arms. Our solar system is located on a small area that is between the two major arms.

OUR SOLAR SYSTEM

## OUR NEIGHBOR

The Andromeda Galaxy is our closest spiral galaxy. The Milky Way and the Andromeda Galaxy are moving toward each other at about 70 miles per second. In about 4 billion years, the two galaxies will merge and combine into one big galaxy.

ANDROMEDA GALAXY

The word galaxy comes from the Greek gala, which means milk.

## THE SPINNING SOLAR SYSTEM

The Milky Way rotates continuously, and our solar system moves with it at an average speed of 515,000 miles per hour. Even though that's unbelievably fast, the solar system would take approximately 230 million years to travel all the way around the Milky Way!

The Sun has made 16 complete revolutions around the Milky Way since it was formed about 4.5 billion years ago.

## WHY IT IS CALLED THE MILKY WAY ?

Ancient people looked up at the night sky and saw a streak of white light. They referred to this, our galaxy, as a path, a river, and as milk, so this galaxy became named the Milky Way.

# GLOSSARY

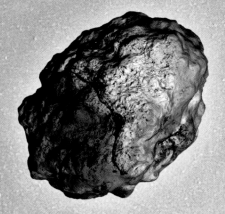

**Atmosphere:** the mass of gases surrounding a planet or moon

**Comet:** a celestial body made of ice and dust that develops a cloudy tail as it orbits closer to the Sun

**Constellation:** a particular or recognizable pattern of a group of stars

**Asteroid:** a large, irregularly shaped rocky body that orbits the Sun

**Astronaut:** someone who is trained to travel in spacecraft in outer space

**Aurora:** streams of colored light that move across the sky in polar regions, caused by solar flares interacting with Earth's magnetic field

**Axis:** the imaginary line through the center of a planet around which it rotates

**Crater:** a large, circular impression made on the surface of a planet or moon, caused by a meteorite impact

**Eclipse:** the partial or complete blocking of a planet, star, sun, or moon by another body

**Galaxy:** a massive group of stars, planets, gas, and dust

**Gravity:** the force of attraction between objects that depends on their mass

**Light-year:** a unit of distance that light travels in one year (5,880,000,000,000 miles)

**Mass:** the amount of matter in an object

**Meteor:** a small body of matter from outer space that may glow for a short time from the heat as it enters Earth's atmosphere

**Meteoroid:** a meteor that orbits the Sun

**Orbit:** the path of a planet, moon, comet, or spacecraft around another body, such as a planet, moon, or star

**Revolution:** the completion of an orbit by a planet, moon, or comet

**Rotation:** a complete turn

**Shooting Star:** the visible path of a meteoroid as it enters Earth's atmosphere

**Solar System:** a group of planets, asteroids, comets, and moons that orbit a star. Our solar system is made up of eight planets (Mercury, Venus, Earth, Mars, Jupiter, Saturn, Uranus, and Neptune) and their moons, as well as asteroids and comets that orbit the Sun

**Supernova:** the explosion of a very large star that gives off massive amounts of energy

**Terrestrial:** of, on, or relating to land

**Universe:** all the space, matter, and energy in existence

# INDEX